# ON EAGLE'S WINGS

# KATE BRUMBY

Written by Kate Brumby
Copyright Kate Brumby 2019
Text copyright © Kate Brumby
Cover Created by Webleo

All rights reserved. No part of this publication may be reproduced, stored in a retrieval system, transmitted or copied in any form or by any means, electronic, mechanical, photocopying, recording or otherwise, without the prior written permission of the copyright owner.

The moral right of the Author has been asserted.

Contact: hello@katebrumby.co.uk

Isaiah 40:31

But those who hope in the Lord will renew their strength.
They will soar on wings like eagles;
they will run and not grow weary,
they will walk and not be faint.

New International Version

# Foreword

*Solace in my mind was my longing*
*This the echo of my heart's lament*
*Every waking hour pulling emotions*
*Dreams fractured unceasingly turbulent.*
*Restless and devoid of peace within*
*Nothing appeared to console or appease*
*Until with utter despair and submission*
*Convicted I fell suddenly to my knees.*
*Realising I had tried too hard, too long*
*To be my own protector and guide*
*I'd ignored the yearning for another*
*Someone to trust and in confide.*
*Contrite tears fell from my eyes so freely*
*Not held back, there was no longer need*
*I realised that the release of myself*
*Was the only way to solace and peace.*
*He gently drew near to be beside me*
*Careful to not scare or wilfully intrude*
*Just close enough for me to be aware*
*So when ready towards Him I'd move.*

*God and I have both moved during 2020 – to a place that feels closer than ever before. We have spent many hours together. Writing has lifted my spirit and kept me going.*
*I pray that God will draw close to you in coming days and lift you to soar as if on the wings of eagles.*

Kate

# 1

We have been granted freedom to act
To choose which path of life to pick
Perhaps not an easy one in truth
But I have decided to follow His.
The Way of Life acknowledging God
And of His gift of Life itself
Knowing deep within my heart
My need of Him above anything else.
I ask that He would guide me
Continually request He'd me hone
Today and in the days yet to be
Before He calls me to His Home.

## 2

In each step taken we are reminded
you've gone before
And You're beside us helping us
barriers to conquer.
Nothing or anyone can or should be
compared to you
No other had the power to truly get us
safely through.
Faith is tested daily, emotions in some
held taut
Relationships tested and households
clearly fraught.
Anger and frustration heightened and
some contained
Others anxious and feeling
overwhelmed and afraid.
Lord, draw near and be our one refuge
and strength
In this and in each moment may You
calm please send.
Lord, may we all be enabled to do all
that we can
For our own sake and for that of our
fellow man.

## 3

Lord, as we walk towards Jerusalem
May we be unafraid of what others think
May our focus be on You alone, Lord
As our faults and needs to You bring.
May we be mindful of our path beginning
That You will take time to each of us hone
As into our hearts and our minds, Lord
You in Your grace make here your home.
May this Holy Week be one of reassurance
That we stand not alone or in fear
As we remember Your promise of hope
That You will be always to us near.
May this Easter be a transformation,
As each of us on bended knee says
"Lord, forgive all that is past and gone
Thank you that by Your blood I'm saved".

## 4

Prayers, my thoughts offered up to You
Prayers, my hopes that You'll get me through
Prayers, my joy as I say "thanks so much"
As You answer with Your generous love.
Prayers, the questions that I sometimes ask
Prayers, the anxieties and worries I have
Prayers, my calmness that comes to appease
As You answer with Your gift of peace.
Prayers, I hold up my family and my friends
Prayers, said at day beginning and at its end
Prayers, the way I acknowledge You, my Lord
As my heart speaks more than any word.

## 5

Lord within the day You are with me
From break of dawn to eventide
Never am I separated or alone
You are there close by my side.
Amongst the wakening of songbirds
I hear Your voice calling me too
A gentle whisper of greeting
As I enter the world anew.
The flower heads turn upwards
As sunrise emits its rays
And I turn to Your Word, Lord
To see what You have to say.
I hold Your book before me
Ready to receive Your wisdom
And then place it down again
Equipped for the day to begin.
At close of night I reflect too
Grateful for all You've bestowed
I sleep in peace and security
Enriched by what I've been told.
One day turns into another
Yet I do not tire - I am at ease
For with You each moment
I feel an incredible peace.

## 6

Hear my prayer of supplication, Lord
Be with those who are ill and near death
Stay close to reassure the sick who're afraid
May you defuse feelings of being bereft.
Hear my prayer for those who nurse and treat
As with deep sorrow their hearts are torn
Guard them from harm dear Lord
Be close so that they are not forlorn.
Hear my prayer for family and loved ones
Who are unable to be where they wish to
Allow your Angels to be alongside them
Aiding their grief and barriers to get through.
Hear my prayer of quiet upholding
As I know not what words to say
May You be within each and all in need
Hear and act, Lord I humbly pray.

## 7

Continue to teach me Lord
Of the humility of You in Christ
Give me the wisdom to pause
When responding to think twice.
To ever be mindful of others
Of the things they can share
And if I am open to listen
To the many truths I can learn.
May I be someone who's humble
And willing to help someone else
Remembering all are equal
As I think less of myself.
No one has more importance
Each has status and worth
And in showing love and respect
I also You through them serve.
May this Maundy Thursday
Be a continuation of action
Command to serve all others
And of my life a commendation.

## 8

On the same night as He was betrayed
He took bread and gave thanks
He also blessed the wine
Taking each in His hands.
Those same hands bore pain
The pain of His crucifixion
As he took my place upon the cross
The cost for my salvation.
Yet, He continues to accept me
Though I daily betray and fail
Yet, He continues to forgive me
Though each sin strikes another nail.
I gaze upon my crucified Lord
And I am in awe as I watch
His hands stretched out before me
He says, "I love you this much".
From *In the Palm of His Hand* ©2019

## 9

As I stand at the foot of the cross
I watch as they carry your body away
As I am left not knowing the future
I am drawn to my knees to pray.
As I spend the night being restless
I ache for all that has now gone
As I see the darkness being lifted
I look upward to see the new dawn.
As I dare to venture to look closer
I am in awe of Your work at hand
As I recall the prophecies of the past
I am struck by details You planned.
As I consider the world of this Easter
I know without doubt You're in control
As I wait on Holy Saturday evening
I know that all in You is possible.

## 10

"I am the resurrection" says the Lord
"You have Eternal Life through Me
Though your earthly body will be no more
You will from finite death be free.
One day you will join Us
Father, Son, and Holy Ghost
Just as I have always promised
Then to abide in heavenly realms.
There will be great rejoicing
As you come to your God above
You'll experience a consuming awareness
Of My power, compassion and love.
Your eyes will be fully opened
My glory you will completely see
You will listen with new ears
And your lips only good will speak.
Look forward to the day of Our union
But be sure the date only I know
Before you and I meet face to face
On Earth you must continue to grow.
I have allocated jobs for you
I have carefully chosen each one
And only when all are finished
Will I then bring you Home."

## 11

To seek to do good each day
Is what my Lord asks of me
Reassured He's my refuge
And one day His face I'll see.
There will be trials ahead
There'll be those who scorn
But He who is my example
Will teach them also in turn.
God will reveal His purposes
He will help the weak stand
Aiding each along their walk
With the guidance of His hand.
Never will He forsake, not ever
He will be the one that is true
The one to rely upon in all
Victorious for me and for you.

## 12

My heart was torn when He spoke to me
Aching emotions to the words I heard
"Do not doubt but believe, My friend,
Put your finger and hand there".
A week before I'd dismissed others
Telling them their news was false
Then perplexed and yet so excited
Incredibly there I saw for myself.
I know not why I had questioned
My humanness I guess over took
I needed the evidence before me
My own eyes upon wounds to look.
I do believe, how could I now not?
Yes, I hear His commission now too,
To go and tell others of the gospel,
Forgiveness , new Life and the Truth!

## 13
Walking alone is not possible
There is One who is ever by my side
He also stands in my corner
And wipes away tears I cry.
Oppressors have no power
He alone is stronger than all
Ever ready to delight in me
I am without doubt evermore.

## 14
It's foolish to think I am blameless
Devoid of all guilt and shame
It is only through Christ I am washed
By His sacrifice and His holy name.
Nothing I do can make amends
Only You are my Deliverer, my Aid
It is before You I am prostrate
My inner weakness here laid.
Restoration is my only plea
Forgiveness and eternal life to know
Purge me of all wretchedness
Come Lord, come to me below.
Rescue me and rejoice my Lord
Once lost I am now found in You
Willing and wanting to now live
Denouncing the old for the new.

## 15

To be a 'beacon' within this world
Be it of hope of life or of love
To be those who strive
Always to do what we should.

What better legacy could there be?
What greater medal to attain?
Than to know our bidding is right
And for it the world is changed.

The part we play may not be known
Not made public or publicised
But it is not what man looks upon
Importance is seen by God's eyes.

May I seek to do good deeds
For others to be prepared to act
Not just letting everyone else move
And on my own laurels just sit back.

May within my corner of this world
I do something to honour Him
Whether prayer or word to reassure
And as a Christian be witnessing.

May my actions be productive
Sewing, knitting or telephone call
May I end each day knowing
That I could have done no more.

May in sleep as in relaxation, Lord
Your grace be given to all who serve
So that each tomorrow yet to come
Each will give again in full worth.

Not half hearted or with resistance
May You provide what is required
The joy, peace and impetus for all
In mine and in all others' lives.

## 16
Moment by moment that is all
That is all I need to take
Step by step by step too
Each one at a time to make.
When life is hard I can rely
Upon You to lift me up
To be with me going forward
Avoiding decisions to stop.
I thank You Lord for courage
When life is difficult for me
I thank you for reassurance
When my future I cannot see.
May I ever walk on with You
Unafraid of what others think
May I be refreshed this night
Ready for tomorrow to begin.

## 17

Lord reassure when I doubt and know
not what to say
Lord listen to my heart rather than the
words I pray
Lord keep me within the shadow of
Your wings
Lord hold me close in my activities and
my resting.
Lord show me for whom you'd have
me think of
Lord guide me to those who are finding
life tough
Lord grant me the comfort of knowing
You're there
And that all You protect in Your loving
care.

## 18

My feet upon the rock need to stand
Not upon the sands that move beneath
To welcome God's living Word to be
Within every breath that I now breathe.
To be equipped I need to learn
And ask for His guidance to know
For in dwelling within His scriptures
I will become wise and clearly grow.
He will provide all that is required
In the battles ahead that I face
He will be alongside me each step
Never once turning away His face.
Lord of my being and of my future
God will deliver me safe at last
My blessed assurance and foothold
Just as sure now as in the past.

## 19

Within the Word set before me
I see what's needed to do my best
Precepts and guidance there
Teachings to provide joy and rest.
Warnings in times of danger
Commandments to me protect
A way of life to live here and now
Promise of eternity with You next.
A world in which I find myself
Is but a transient place for me
For one day I know for sure
No doubt, I feel only certainty.
May my eyes be truly opened
May my feet walk in rhythm too
May my tongue be ever guarded
And my ways be free of evil.

## 20

The winds of change and tides of time
Bid each of us to kneel and pray
Upon the shore of the unknown
Asking You dear Lord to us save.
Place Your wisdom within the minds
Of those who make important decisions
That mankind and Your Kingdom here
Would rid the world of all divisions.
None focused on ego or self importance
Not wishing their pride to grow or gain
But for the best for the people in each nation
May they too also kneel here and pray.
All one voice and one expectation
The world restored to where it should be
All health and equality clearly evident
No servanthood or any disparity.
Gladly may we all stand together soon
In our walk forward be united in Truth
Assured and confident all battles are won
When in faith we put our trust in You.

## 21

You go before me and in doing so prepare
You go alongside me here and everywhere.
You go so that I am reassured I'm not alone
You go with me each moment, each tomorrow.
You go and I try to follow, I try to you emulate
You go and I follow in and to strengthen my faith.
You go and I ask You to teach me to deeply trust
You go and I am reminded of the depth of Your love.
You go yet no further away than a heart beat
You go yet as close as a breath that I breathe.
You go yet inwardly no space between You and I
You go not anywhere in my life or when I die.

## 22

Lord, remind me that all are precious
and life is a gift
Lord, remind me that but for Your
grace I may feel adrift.
Lord, show me via the heart within who
needs me this day
Lord, show me what I can do and
provide the words to say.
Lord, help me be able and willingly to
give of my time
Lord, help me without reserve the lost
to help find.
Lord, in reflection may I hold up all in
prayer to You
Lord, may I not underestimate what all
are going through.
Lord, within the darkness provide the
light we all need
Lord, within the darkness may you
shine hope for us to see.
Lord, may You be the answer to the
questions we each ask
Lord, may You be our strength in all we
are now tasked.

## 23

My shepherd and my Provider
My comfort and source of strength
May my life be honourably lived
From now until my journey's end.
Take my heart and lead me onwards
Towards pastures rich in Your love
Guided there to reach out to others
As You have taught that I should.
Banish regrets and unworthiness
Let me be Your servant henceforth
Dwelling with You here on Earth
And also in Heaven for evermore.

## 24

Standing before me I picture You
A huge smile upon your face
A welcome greeting from me
And from You a warm embrace.

Instantly we'd all feel at ease
You'd enter gladly our home
And we'd sit together happily
As You made it Your own.

There'd be no need to impress
You'd accept everything and all
We'd offer cake and tea of course
And ask if You need anything more.

Time would pass oh so quickly
On leaving You'd again us hug
And our house would also know
Of Your incredible love.

Nothing would your visit eclipse
Except the time we first met
That remains my heart's memory
Forever within seeded and set.

My abode doesn't have walls, no
Nor a driveway or any doors
My soul lives within my being
But You know that of course.

With each heartbeat You are there
Each breath I breathe there too
There's been no distance for years
I am forever connected to You.

I pray others would You welcome
Into homes but more so their hearts
All they need do is ask You in
Then You take up Your own part.

You'll grant forgiveness and peace
You'll provide console and compassion
As all who say, "My Lord please enter"
Become Your disciple, a Christian.

## 25

Lord, in Your mercy redeem this Your world
Make new all upon its oceans and plains
Come with Your healing power O Lord
Restore the Earth's nations once again.
Hold nothing back as You enter hearts
Completely take hold and embrace us
So that our responses are whole too
Putting in You our lives and our trust.
May Your Kingdom come in fullness
So the world is forever now changed
As each of us humbly repents and says,
"Thank you, Jesus I praise Your name".

## 26

To dwell in Your presence O Lord
Is my yearning and my heart's desire
To stand upon level ground upright
Impassioned with hope and Your fire.
I will sing a song of thanksgiving
Raising my voice and hands aloft
No longer held back by wrongdoing
As I taste and receive of Your cup.
My joy I know will be overflowing
Your fullness generously given me
As I trust in You Lord unwavering
My whole being will soar above free.

## 27

To be patient requires willingness
A willingness to be still and to wait
Not rushing on or even nudging along
It is a time to savour and contemplate.
To be patient is like taking a pause
So that the whole can be considered
A few moments to problem solve
So a solution can be reconfigured.
Not giving up is about patience
As is resolve and drive to carry on
When I think of many circumstances
It's with resolution that they've begun.
Resolution to seek a clearer picture
Resolution to have an aim and a plan
Resolution to accept divergence
Resolution to always keep calm.
Lord teach me to be faithful and patient
Guard me from giving up or giving in
Help me be resolved in all that I do
May this time here be strengthening.

## 28

Lord, my strength and my Shepherd
My portion and the trust of my heart
I lift my pleas and praise to You
As this day I rise up and start.
I have many trials ahead of me
But I am consoled that You're here
Walking by my side continually
And so I need not now fear.
You will not despise or forsake me
You will hear my pleas deep within
In every fraction You'll heal
And I Your child will strengthen.
Reward will be my blessing
Praise the song I sing in delight
Held up by Your victorious arms
Rescued from my human plight.

## 29

May You give strength to all who are weakened
May there be hope in the days to yet be
May You bless each and every nation
With Your healing and immeasurable peace.
May we rise up and stand together united
May we see Your Kingdom now here come
May all needs be met without reservation
With everyone finding in You their home.
May there be an incredible celebration
May there be console and compassion too
May the true beacon of all Light dear Lord
Be seen and as acknowledged as being You.

## 30

Flamboyant in hues of an array of colours
Hope is what all look for in each day
Light at the end of the tunnel we're in
Answers to the prayers that we pray.
There is a yearning of someone to rescue
To put an end to the darkness once and for all
For the might and strength of God Himself
To return in His majestic power once more.
One day He will indeed be amongst us
His reign will be throughout the world
But in the meantime we are to do His work
As His disciples and witnesses are called.
We can be and are His beacons of Light
Hope is given to us to speak of too
As I walk along the path before me now
I am ready to do my part - are you?
There is strength in numbers, there's truly,

Together there's no limit to
achievement
As Colonel Tom sings 'You'll never
walk alone'
I salute him in sincere complete
agreement.
We and others need to stand up, be
counted
To walk as Colonel Tom has indeed
done
Faith and belief both sure and certain
This day, and in all the days yet to come.

## 31

I receive console knowing You are near
Within each day there are discoveries
I receive countless blessings, Lord
Which by far outweigh any anxieties.
Upon the wings of hope ascending
I cannot help but in awe be amazed
That within the shadows of this world
You bring Light to each and every day.
In the stillness of my expectation
Your voice is soft and oh so very clear
"My child, take courage, be patient
None amongst you need now fear.
I will rise up and my power will reign
My glory others will in time really see
But as yet, I have not named the day
For this you must wait patiently".

## 32

To trust in You, my own dear Lord
To walk along knowing You're here
To with a hopeful heart beating
To in faith to You move ever near.
To watch and wait with expectation
To visualise Your glory upon the Earth
To know without shadow of doubt
I am to You of immeasurable worth.
To rest knowing You never sleep, Lord
To stand secure in Your hand I'm held
To mindfully live in each moment
In Your Word to have anxieties consoled.
These are the prayers for others I have
Along with myself I leave at Your cross
Asking again that Your Kingdom come
As in You I put the whole of my trust.
These are the prayers for myself too
My hope is in You and You alone
Remembering the promise to Noah
That of Your vow seen in the rainbow.

## 33

Take me and use me Lord
In the bidding of Your hand
With your confidence
Help me walk and stand.
Guide me as my Shepherd
Your voice clear and firm
So I may understand
And from Your Word learn.
Provide all that I need
To become Your servant
Let nothing deter me
Nor any barrier prevent.
May my hope remain in You
As each step I take onward
Seeking to be obedient
And no other reward.
Instil in me discipline
A willing and open heart
In the next hours, Lord
As a new chapter I start.

## 34

Lord You've taken all my uncertainty
And guided my next steps and moves
You have taken feeling of puzzlement
And drawn me closer towards You.
Lord You're guarding my heart
So I don't feel fearful or anxious
You are holding my hand closely
Increasing daily my love and trust.
Lord You prompt prayerful reflection
To remind me to pray for others' needs
You provide reassurance and console
As prayers bring with them unease.
If I dwell upon the realities dear Lord
Of all those ill, bereaved and bereft
I know it would be beyond my capacity
And emotionally I'd find it too much.
I will continue of course to pray
For loved ones and strangers too
Asking for Your Kingdom to come.

## 35

Lord, upon the wings of Eagles
Prayers are raised upwards to You
With requests for console, Father
Your eyes to see others through.
For hearts to be softened, Lord
Stones melted with Your touch
As each moment that's yet to be
You stoop to us with Your love.
I ask for grace and gratitude
For Your blessings in my life
And deeper awareness Lord
Of those who suffer and strive.
May I be reminded of context
Of what's important and what's not
Assured that my own sin done
Is so quickly by You forgot.
May I too be accepting, Lord
Not holding grudge or on to pain
Dwelling on recriminations
Willingly from this day refrain.
So on closing of night dear Lord
I pray for all nations and the world
Asking Your Kingdom to come
And a united people You'd build.

## 36

Beneath the shadows of Your wings
We have the choice to safely abide
Within the shadows of falsehood
We have the choice to there hide.
For some no decision is ever made
They are forced and robbed of youth
Some are imprisoned and tormented
Others beaten, tortured and abused.
Light can seem so far off from them
In a relentless spiral of little hope
There will be some who fail or die
Unable in their situation to cope.
A glimpse into this world of depravity
Will have changed me for evermore
Unable to erase what was seen
Never again its true reality ignore.
For those who have looked as I have
I pray that they and I will do something
For those who are part of the picture
Your kingdom to come I am calling.
Soon, Lord I ask soon You'd heal
You'd restore each child to be a child
So that all would be assured of safety
And beneath Your wings together abide.

## 37

Held within Your palm dear Lord
There's a stillness that abounds
A quiet understanding here
With hardly an audible sound.
Yet Your voice is clear and gentle
As You speak direct to my soul
Reassuring me of Your presence
Providing what You wish me know.
The pages of Your Word, Lord
Are full of solace and of care
No matter what my circumstance
I find answers available there.
Each day that passes I'm drawn
Wanting to understand and be fed
Eager to discover more of You
To read, to pray and to reflect.
I begin this my day in hope, Lord
With my request in Your prayer
Thy Kingdom come and will be done
In this moment please and forever.

## 38

All within the world united
No one greater in worth
Joined with equal hearts
Creating heaven on Earth.
Inner voices audible
As together we all stand
Praise, worship and singing
Vocally and with our hands.
Reminded none are different
Fundamentally all are the same
Locked down for a time
Until we're able to meet again.

## 39

When I sit with You, Lord
I'm reminded of inequalities
Of the way man treats man
And of world's disparities.
I ask that You'd give wisdom
As the past You forgive
Guiding me to play my part
With social conscience live.
To take time to consider
What and how I buy goods
And for origins and *Fairtrade*
To search for and to look.
May others change their ways
Wages, rights, and conditions
This is my prayer, our Father
This is my sincere petition.

## 40

Lord, hear my prayers and songs voiced
Hear the meanings signed and spoken too
May we worship in true unity here, Lord
Giving petition and our praise to You.
May we hold nothing back in reluctance
Grant us hearts that are open ready to speak
And in the silence in which You enter us
Pour Your Spirit upon all to safely us keep.
Let us be people who recognise one another
Not as different or unable to understand
Build Your children with true fellowship, Lord
A family held together in the palm of Your hand.

## 41

Reflected memories linger
As melodies upon the air
Taking us back to times gone
Wishing we were now there.
But hope is ever strengthened
As optimism breaks through
Looking forward to good times
Making of memories that are new.

## 42

Within the day of your bidding
I stand firm upon the ground
Unwavering in conviction
Regardless of what I find.
There are potholes to trip
Hazards hinder regularly
But nothing I've encountered
Has distanced You from me.
My Lord You are ever closer
So I am not alone or fearful
Together we walk onwards
Down valleys and up hills.
May I remain faithful, Lord
Holding Your strong hand
Moving along the path ahead
Just as You have planned.
Guard my mind from worries
Help my heart beat as Yours
In harmony and rhythm
United in one true course.
Prayerful may I listen
Wisdom please me bestow
In this day at this time
And in each new tomorrow.

## 43

My hope is in the Lord, my God
Upon His Word I focus my mind
I ask for His voice to guide me
On His wisdom I now rely.
I request He keep me safely
And also others that I love
Holding each within His hand
As I raise my prayers to Him above.
My God's gentle reassurance daily
I pause and take time to enjoy
Whilst filling days with activity
In interesting things employed.
Little opening for doubt or fear
To enter my heart or my head
No thoughts of anxiety or worry
Nor anticipation of dread.
Being in the moment I linger
Resting before moving on
But later this day I'll return
To God's Word to again come.
Hope will be my motto hourly
Positive and realistic Truth say
Remembering He is ever with me
No more than a prayer away.

## 44

Lord, as in the world you made each one
Different from the next and unique
There is much to learn from one another
In the way we live and seek a peace.


Common amongst us our needs, Lord
Whatever they are, we wish them met
Many determined to help themselves
Thankfully some on generosity set.


There are those who give without asking
Relentless offering time, skills, wealth
Some of course continue self focused
Thinking little of or aiding no one else.


May I be mindful, Lord of your bidding
And listen to Your voice within speak
So that my hands and actions tomorrow
Will be response to where You lead.

Make my heart ever softer, Lord
Guard me from selfishness and pride
Keep me from ignoring others' needs
Help me to be proactive and kind.


May this night be a time of realignment
As humaneness evolves and explodes
So that all will indeed become equal
In this Your developing new world.

## 45

Words linger and then come rushing
Eager to place themselves down here
Forever lost and forgotten if delayed
My deliberate dismiss of them they fear.

They are sure of what is to be said
For they come with ease and flow
It is I that am unaware of meaning
Until the verse created they me show.

I write in real time and so very freely
Few pauses are there as I here type
Sentences form with little effort
Though not all spellings are right.

It is as though this way of speaking
Is an extension of who I am within
And that my communion with God
Is here within verse it can begin.

He tells me of things and directs
He provides wisdom to think upon
He guides my reasoning here
He shows me when I am wrong.

This day He speaks of perfection
Of the need only to do my best
And that when there are errors
He will still my writing bless.

Hearts will be opened by poetry
But none more so than my own
For with me He starts and finishes
Ensuring I rely on Him alone.

I must forget self and let go
Allow His words upon my page
And not be tempted to anticipate
What He is saying at any stage.

I am to trust and be ever faithful
To return day after day after day
To meet with Him here writing
And never forget to humbly pray.

## 46

To dwell within Your presence, Lord
In each moment to rest there within
To be still and to be quiet with You
Not be eager with any of my moving.


Inwardly to allow Your soothing
Outwardly too be pampered somehow
The whole of my being caressed
Here, in this time, here and now.


No need to speak or make a sound
Just 'be' and that alone, dear Lord
As I become aware of oneness
Two yet no separation - in accord.


I find myself drifting so gently
Upon the ebb and flow of a tide
A place of complete harmony
With You to endlessly abide.

I pray as my time to move comes
The mood of the night will remain
Even when asleep and dreaming
You'll reassure me again and again.


May the words of Your blessing
Linger on within my mind and heart
As day ends in just a few hours
And as tomorrow also starts.

## 47

Lord You are close even when not visible
Your words are whispered in a gentle way
The presence of Your Holy Spirit I ask
Would aid me Your compassion say.
May I be willing to listen more fully
To what is, and what is not said
So my responses would be fitting
And my speech by You also led.
Somehow cut through the darkness
As with Your rainbow after the rain
Encouraging all who grieve in death
You are with them in their deep pain.
May on eagle's wings they be lifted
Held up and enfolded by You
Be comforter, advocate and aide
Each moment helping all get through.

## 48

May the words of my mouth be acceptable
I have heard people say before they preach
The importance of talking of You, Lord
For You wish to everyone everywhere reach.
Within my day I ask You to guide me
To show how and what to share with the young
Remembering voices of the past years far flung.
Perhaps I am to write and present?
I am sure You will set me on the right path
For the opportunity to do Your bidding, Lord
You will ensure what I need I will have.
I thank you in advance of what is to come
For all You have prepared in my way
Walking forward trusting in faith I go
Onwards to act in the coming days.

## 49

Yellow hearts of bravery and honour now
Will adorn the dwellings in our streets
They will appear as symbols of loss
As we acknowledge others' grief.
Within the hue of sunshine are shadows
Iconic of loss and so very much more
Symbols of tears and of desolation
Yet hope here too will one day soar.
Upon the wings of eagles You'll come
Lifting each one in Your loving embrace
Holding all with infinite compassion
Accepting and healing with Your grace.
For us our call is to neighbours listen
To pray and to ask for Your deep console
Come Lord, come in power Divine
Within each of our hearts for evermore.

## 50

Teach me Lord the wisdom of inactivity
Time spent in true contemplation and pause
When nothing is listened to or heard
But for the voice that is clearly yours.
Amidst the busy days that are before me
Aid with gentleness a stilling of my soul
So I may experience true thankfulness
As people in my prayers to You I hold.
Take my offering, Lord when words fail me
Listen I ask to the small voice here within
Rescue me from self reliance and pride
For controlling traits so burdening.
Keep me safe from doubt of self, Lord
Provide confidence and yet humility
So I may understand and respond
Receiving and acknowledging graciously.
This night may I be still and silent, Lord
As I reflect on the day I have here spent
Be reassured of my place in the world
And be granted sleep that is deeply content.

## 51

**A**lways willing to listen that's how He is
**C**alm and without complication - simplicity
**C**ommon place and accessible
**E**veryone, everywhere, anytime
**P**rayer is just another word for talking
**T**rust is what is needed to just speak His name.

## 52

As day draws to a close dear Lord
And the tiredness meets my eyes
I have few words to utter here
Somehow they are hard to find.
So I ask that You would come bless
All those I hold up in my prayers
That You'd take each into Your heart
And safely hold them all there.
Lord, may tomorrow be a new day
In which hope would be our joy
In whatever we think upon within
And in every way we are employed.
May we remember to be thankful
And show appreciation in all we have
Then as day draws to a close again
May our hearts be peaceful and glad.

## 53

We celebrate the birth of Christ Jesus,
At Christmas time with great cheer,
We rejoice in His resurrection too,
But what about the rest of the year?
God calls us to make a commitment,
We must love as He loves us,
To be there for one another,
And seek the common good.
Are we walking the road of a Christian?
Is it as agnostic we will stay?
Do we wish to proclaim atheism?
The decision is ours...Which way?
From *In the Palm of His Hand* ©2019

## 54

Lord, as days and weeks keep rolling
The walk we have seems very long
I rely on Your counsel daily
To aid me in keeping strong.
I am thankful that Your grace sufficient
Lifts me in moments of unease
And so my mind remains peaceful
Void of distracting anxieties.
Help me Lord to continue resolved
In my response to what I am asked
Aid me in my daily routine
On Your guidance be ever focused.
Lord, as days and weeks keep rolling
For those who rule the world pray
Asking they'd too seek Your assistance
And in their hearts "Come Lord" , say.

## 55

Lord, in the moments of feeling bruised
Whether by my own hand or another
I ask You draw close in Your grace
And help me to stand and recover.
May I be willing to admit wrongness
To ask You to change my heart within
Prepared to forgive self and others
Of my and their pertaining sin.
Let me learn from troubled times
When conscience pricks my mind
So the right ways to respond to You
I can more easily seek and find.
Take, Lord pride away from me
May I be contrite and open to change
Remembering today is not eternal
Feelings and emotions need not remain.
I need not be weighed down longer
To do so would be in itself wrong
Tomorrow will be a new day and start
Tomorrow strengthened I'll carry on.

## 56

Lord, faced with decisions set before me
In which direction and when to move
I ask that I will be closely guided
As I daily turn my face towards You.
Help me to be sensitive and empathic
So my ears would listen not just hear
Aid as I debate consequences
As I aim to abate anxiety and fear.
Keep me close and reassured, Lord
That I am where I must be this day
Reminding me in love of others
I can show care as for them I pray.
In this time of Thy Kingdom Come
May in power yet gentleness ever be
As those who struggle for wisdom
Pause and look towards You and me.
Me because I am called to be Witness
To all that You show and also say
And who in this verse remind all
To You to turn in all their ways.

## 57

Within the shadows I take my refuge
Hidden there You provide my sanctuary
Allowing rest until the time again comes
To face those who would trample on me
Solace is mine within the shadows
Compassion is Yours along with mercy
I am assured that You will hear my plight
Before releasing me to soar free.
High above those who dishonour
Even there protected always by You
Never alone whatever the challenge
Your Spirit to guide me ever through.

## 58

There is a daily battle upon this our Earth
As the choices we have known become
Many are eager to stand strong for You
Others to instant gratification succumb.
There is much to learn by looking backwards
To the lives gone before our own of today
As we reflectively consider traits exhibited
Of steadfast love and of inconsistent sway.
There are those who provide prime example
Giving us hope in what they like us faced
Who by their determination unfaltering
Point us to God and His blessings and grace.
Perhaps some will not inspire or encourage
As we look upon all they failed in life to do

But even they as part of God's own creation
Somehow tell nothing is too hard to get through.
In loyalty, honour and also in gratitude
Ruth is one who is an example to each and all
As in friendship and unblemished devotion
She could not have done very much more.
Tomorrow may I rise in hope and expectation
Like Ruth prepared to go where I know I must
And equipped with all I need in You my Lord
Not faint nor ever be tempted to give up.

## 59

Yours Lord, is the wonder, the
splendour and the majesty,
All that I am and can be is Yours, and
Yours alone,
In the hours, days, weeks ahead of me,
dear Lord,
I pray that Your Kingdom would
fervently come.

I ask for wisdom and real
understanding for others,
That all would act in ways that are
honourable to all,
None feeling more important or
devalued by another,
As each walks along with the next in
one accord.

I ask You to keep me strong in Your
promises,
Holding me within Your hand
protecting my whole,
Reassured that You are with all whom I
pray
For You have told me clearly this will
be so.

May the hope in You be my beacon ahead, Lord
The light that shows me the way from shadows
Your Word a source of all that I need daily
And in each, in Your grace, the coming tomorrows.

## 60

Within the chaos and unpredictable world we're in
Still the most reliable strength is from You
Nothing can shake the belief we here have
Nor help us with each of the barriers we come to.
Amidst the unknown it is You who beckons
To each heart and mind to be still and know
Of your infinite acceptance and forgiveness
And of your blessings You wish to bestow.
There is nowhere we can hide in the universe
Nothing is unknown to You or lost at all
Everyone and everything here and in the heights
Brings us back to You - whom we really search for.

In looking to the planets, stars, and
even creation
We cannot fail to also see the work of
Your hand
Guiding exploration and new
discoveries
With perfect timing as You alone
could've planned.
The tomorrows will bring hope and
knowledge
We will gain in wisdom, skills and
deeper insight
Mankind will be equipped in the ways
required
To virus, war, unrest, hunger, inequality
to fight.
Eventually all will stand up in complete
union
No one will be thought lesser by
another, no
As Your Kingdom comes in its
completion
World and man restored as it was so
long ago.
Healed in a way that is beyond
comprehension

Each step small yet with great global impact
A new day dawns, as it is promised I know
Looking forward and not dwelling on the past.
Hope is the beacon that lights my path ahead
Believe in a new age and a better life for all
With only one thing required from each of us
Prayers of contrition when You our Lord calls.

## 61

Spirit of Pentecost Sunday
Birth of the God's own Church
Generation of new birth beheld
Commissioned to others touch.
To be His presence with skin on
In a world tossed and torn apart
Many who feel detached now
Grief filling and breaking hearts.
To pray without ceasing forever
Never giving up or turning away
Lifting the needs of neighbours
In faith and faithfulness to pray.
Joyful and celebratory singing
Calm and stillness to listen too
As with all being, mind and soul
Welcomed and strengthened by You.

## 62

Patience and peaceful silence
Is what I need from You Lord
A continued resolve to wait
And Your word and hand hold.
To rest in the reassurance
That You have not or will change
And wherever I am walking
With me You will always remain.
Though the world goes onwards
I will too in a different way
As I listen, reflect and respond
In each of the coming days.
There will be a celebration too
Not overt that others will see
But within my heart as it's honed
By the blessings You give to me.

## 63

Upheld by Your hand dear Lord
Where none can destroy or harm
Reassured within Your protection
My heart and mind filled with calm.
Unfaltering is Your presence
Ever with me from dawn to dusk
Power beyond any earthly being
My stronghold of steadfast love.
Even in the night You are with me
Filling my soul with songs of joy
Secured by Your power eternal
That nothing of man can destroy.

## 64

Lord, within the stillness of this night
In the silence where there're no words
May the truth of equality of all men
As belief and truth be unfurled.
Lord, as hearts of stone are made flesh
Grant understanding of the fact
No skin colour is superior or lower
It is indeed as simple as that!

## 65

**H**olding
**O**ne truth
**P**erpetually
**E**ven when life is hard.

**H**earing
**O**ne voice
**P**ierce
**E**very dark moment.

**H**aving
**O**ne promise
**P**ermanently
**E**ach breath I take.

## 66

In words of praise and exultation
I thank God for all things today
Remembering others less fortunate
As humbly I kneel here to pray.
I ask that He would be gracious
Provide all that is needed by all
Protecting, healing and sustaining
Answering all whose hearts now call.
Grant the world refuge and consolation
Take away sickness and prejudice
Bringing His kingdom amongst us
Making the world and people His.

## 67

How in deep sorrow You appear so close
May not be understood as they look on
But upon the screen broadcast now
Your wisdom, strength is here called upon.
Open hearts are requested in service
Grace and steadfast hope henceforth
The name of Jesus echoes in replies
Three in One needed and nothing more.
Through the praise of those here gathered
May Your Truth and mighty power shine
As You welcome Your repenting children
Saying, "Come, peace, know You are mine."

## 68

Lord, the shadows are where some hide
Unwilling to respond to Your clear call
I too have been reluctant at times
Not truly wanting to listen any more.
You have persevered in Your beckoning
Patiently You have awaited my openness
Knowing in time I would hear and heed
And come to You to receive forgiveness.
I know this is a new beginning for me
As I look upon the world in which I live
Reassured that in the actions required
All needed graciously to me now give.
The next steps we will walk together
Hand in hand bound with a cord
Three strands strong and sufficient
As with the world we move forward.

## 69

Lord of the waters and the sky above
Look upon me in all I pursue
Grant me clarity of thought and word
As I attempt to be of myself true.
Guide the choice of what I will read
The stories I will share too
Hold me Lord this night in rest
Refreshing me for day anew.
In each of the slots of time, Lord
May I be confident and steadfast
Calm and cheerful in delivery
Able to answer questions I'm asked.
May I be mindful of Your blessing
Of words written and in speech
Never taking them for granted
As with grace, humility You teach.
Quieten the hearts and minds ready
So ears may hear Your voice clear
As in blessing You call their name
Drawing towards them and me near.
Lord of the waters and the sky above
Look upon me in all I pursue
Grant me clarity of thought and word
Keep me faithful and true to You.

## 70

Lord, over the years You have guided me
To become all that I am this day
You have listened to my yearnings
In my silence kept all for whom I pray.
Your hand is ever before me
Your grace and generosity bestowed
Making my life rich beyond measure
As more of You I come to know.
Bless all that read Of You here Lord
Grant rest and peace within all
May they, as I know Your presence
Is with them also, now and evermore.

## 71

Dear Lord when my strength is spent
And I am tired and weary of mind
I pray You will still my soul gently
So I may refreshment within find.
Help me, Lord to not rush in action
Guide me to be patient and wait
And be open to Your message
That will console and placate.
May I learn from the challenges
Which come along my path here
And always be assured, O Lord
Of Your presence being ever near.

## 72

I hope the window to my soul
Is of a kind and gentle hue
An inviting image to the eye
Providing a welcoming view.
I hope the window to my heart
Is both strong and resilient
Not easily broken or damaged
My faith being transparent.
I hope the window to my life
Is compliant, and with purpose
Lived how God would like to be
And void of being ostentatious.

## 73

It is said by David, the Psalmist and Poet,
That we are all fearfully and wonderfully made,
That nothing in our lives is without purpose,
Early on in my own life this was plain.
God knew and knows the days before me,
And as I look back I see His detailed plan,
The unexpected blessing of now writing,
Was already etched on the palm of His hand.
The words that flow in real time capture,
The gift that God in His wisdom bestowed,
In such a way that my words here now,
Must come from Him, and Him alone.

## 74

The Psalm is a plea for help.
Lord who reigns over land and sea
Over fire and drought have power
I ask that You would be raised up
As mankind bows and becomes lower.
In pardon and deliverance
May all look upon You in deep awe
Realising that actions without You
Are momentary and nothing more.
May men, women and all children
Recognise You the sustainer of all
And for Your help and actions, Lord
In Jesus' name now to You call.
Rise up Your people and world
Making all new as it was at the first
Rebooted so to speak to Creation
And no longer by evil here cursed.

## 75

My Lord as this day draws to an end
I look back on what I have done
In seeing those I have met and to
spoken
I pray that I have shared Your own love.

In each of the days yet to come
In Your grace I ask You'd soften my
heart
So I would not be afraid to reach out
And be ever ready to play my own part.

I ask that You'd make my life Your own
That I would willingly be Your hands
To hold the weak and lonely up
For justice and rights for all to stand.

Help me, Lord make each day count
Not mindlessly waste time or chance
Grateful for those placed in my path
May I aid them with Your confidence.

## 76

Mighty Deliver of power I see
With shield and sword at Your side
The armour that You chose for me
When war against evil I here find.
I also see Your Word O Lord
Greater in strength than any axe
Faced with trials and tribulations
It is the Truth that me attracts.
Soothed by all that is within here
Equipped to face man full on
Enfolded by Your Spirit now
I am where I know I belong.
Unshaken I stand firm Lord
Nothing will sever this tie
You are mine and I am Yours
In Life I will not ever die.

## 77

Lord within the stillness of this day
Within the quiet of the morn I am
Asking for Your presence with me
To enable me to do that which I can.
Provide, dear Lord a thirst and hunger
So that I am drawn to Your feet
Kneeling in humility and wonder
Eager in Your Word to You meet.
Help me Lord to not rush onwards
Soothe my urge and calm my repose
Helping me read now steadily
And listen to what You'd have me know.
May the sentences upon the pages
Become daily Your bread of Life
Remembering all I have needed
You generously in Your love provide.
Teach me so I may be stronger
In the faith that I hereby profess
Aid my understanding, Lord
So others through me may be blessed.
Send me, Lord into the world
Ready to do what I now can
For Your sake for myself I ask,
And in mercy for my fellow man.

## 78

Lord, upon Your children You lavish goodness
To provide Words to teach Your ways
Yet, faced with decisions and judgements
From Your guidance we choose to turn away.


The precepts that You have here provided
Tell of how You would like our lives to be
Asking each to consider applications
And to respond in love and sincerity.


To treat with respect each of our neighbours
As we walk forward along the path ahead
Not looking for the raising up of self, no,
But to seek Your motive and agenda instead.

Lord, take that which has bruised and scarred
Place Your healing balm upon it and me
So that I may learn from experience
And live this day unmarred and joyfully.

## 79

The places within this world
That we individually here fit
Are as a picture in a puzzle
That without one is not complete.
I may not know why I am as I am
But I celebrate that which is not known
And will try to do my part, lord
Until the day You lead me home.

## 80

Much is difficult to cope with now
Within the world in which we live
But I am more and more convinced
That God has much He wants to give.
He is waiting for hearts to be flesh
To turn from being that of stone
For all with one voice He longs
Us to say "Thy Kingdom Come".
It is my prayer as evening ends
That there would be a surge on Earth
As one and then another awakes
In mind and spirit having new birth.
May the joy of all creation exclaim
United in peace and vision here
Not only bid You come dear Lord
But Your voice clearly now hear.
May the hope that is ever in You
Resound in songs of praise afar
As everything on Earth and Heaven
Praises in proclaiming alleluia!

## 81

Music fills the air my Lord
As if to silence the voice within
An outward distraction to me
The focus of my wrestling.
Come in the pauses I ask You
Hear my pleas above the noise
Ignore the chaos and discord
Come Lord, come draw close.
May there be sweet refrain now
Break through to calm all
Lord, my life's composer
Resolve conflict for evermore.

## 82

Word of God speaks to me
In a way like never before
An open page welcomes me
As it were a literal door.
Will I be eager to enter in?
Only time will itself say
There's reluctance to open
Yet eagerness to read the page.
I ask Lord that You'd guide
As each passage I come to
Help me to discern the way
Hearing Your voice of Truth.
Walk with me as I journey
Help me to deeper explore
Your Word and wisdom seek
As in faith I learn more.

## 83

Lord, within the stillness and quiet
I hear Your voice calling my name
Reassuring me You are ever near
And to all ages will remain the same.
Waiting upon You dear Lord
I need not be troubled I now know
For in each step I take forward
You ahead of me surely do go.
You prepare those to whom I speak
You make ready my ears to hear
Your never failing love lifts me up
As Your precepts are made clear.
Promises and vows you'll keep
In calling me by my own name
Yesterday, and today, my God
And forever You'll be the same.

## 84

Wisdom in knowing when to be still
Observant enough to avoid looking
Reliable and resilient so that
Disagreements are not loaded with
Superfluous statements
Openness to mentoring and
Firmly rooted in faith
Grateful and generous words
Reveal the sincerity of heart
Actions of humility
Create a world where everyone is
Equal and valued.

## 85

The world in which we live is moving
In a way that it has never before done
As if this time of change and challenge
Is a way of having a reset button.
Opportunities to be different
More inclusive, equal and fair
Chance to sincerely reach out to all
With generosity and with deep care.
I ask Lord I would do my part now
Not shy away from what You ask me
To speak and to welcome everyone
Giving of myself in Your love freely.
May I not pause too long to consider
But be ready to be Your hand to hold
If not physically, then metaphorically
So no one is left out in the cold.
As I go to rest my dear, Lord, please
May those who need reassurance know
That they are prayed for in this moment
And in You are never ever alone.

## 86

Lord, may I give You all of my heart
Not holding anything here back
Lord, provide for me the courage
When to be brave, confidence I lack.
Take all I am and am yet to be
Nurture me and keep me strong
Reassuring me that I am Yours
And with You I always belong.
Grant me humility in my walking
Keep my eyes fixed just on You
Helping me be resilient in adversity
And able all circumstance get through.
May my gentleness grow now
As with grace I accept Your gift
A newness in my soul given
To afresh each day hereby live.
Looking back may I carry lessons
Wisdom gained celebrate
Certain that only when ready
You'll call me to Heaven's gate.
Until then let me walk on
Along the path You have set ahead
Knowing in Your Word is all
I need to be perfectly led.

## 87

With joy and thanksgiving
Glorious things are spoken of
Every good blessing received
From You my all, my God.
Oh that I would be bold
To stand up and clearly declare
Sovereign Lordship is Yours
Over all peoples everywhere.
May I speak yet tenderly
That my tone be well received
As I thank You publicly
Of how You have blessed me.

## 88

Behold, God makes a new world
Hope is ours in Him alone
He is welcoming all to Himself
In hearts wanting now His home.
All we need do is to be open
Let Him dwell within us freely
Reassured of His faithfulness
And acceptance of us completely.
Offering His hand He says, "Come
Let Me be Yours, and You mine,
So in the places of darkness
Together we can brightly shine".
If you'd like to respond to Him
It is simple in reply say "yes"
He will draw you ever closer
And forever Your life He'll bless.

## 89
Steadfast, true and faithful
God of detail and of His word
Preparing His people to move
As each one will be called.
Hope will fill each nation
Joy released in all hearts
Courageously united standing
Ready to do their own part.
None will be abandoned
Or neglected or cast aside.
We will gather as one, watch
Walking onward side by side.

## 90

If we build with justice, mercy, humility
Everyone's voice will be clearly heard
One will easily love another too
It will be more difficult to or be hurt.

Opinions, attitudes and indifference
Need to be challenged for progress
If there's inward unconscious bias
We need to be willing to now confess.

My prayer is Lord You'd aid us all
To have humble posture in our deeds
When convicted of our weaknesses
Look to You for what we each need.

Lord may Your favour be upon us
As You move throughout this land
May Your peace and will be present
As Your people together now stand.

## 91

Protection is what You provide
No moment without You I spend
You are behind, before and with
The One I can rely on, fully depend
No matter what the future holds
Wherever my path ahead leads
You will be with me throughout
As close as the air that I breathe.

## 92

Taking lessons learnt forward
Celebrating present and the past.
All have potential to be developed
To be changed for good or bad

Freedom is the openness of someone
A willing heart made flesh not stone
In which God's Holy Spirit enters
To within find and make His home.

As God, three in One, begins work
His glory is seen as bright light
Outwardly visible to all looking
As with His touch we are made wise.

Life and living collides anew
An explosion of joy and love,
Shining from our faces turning,
To point others to God above.

## 93

Within the busy days of words and noise
Time to be still is what I know I need
A few hours of being in the moment
In which my soul I patiently hope to feed.
I ask God to take my thoughts and quieten
Leaving me centered and rooted in Him
So that true recharging refreshment
Can in the silence soak within.
Even a short period is welcomed
No rushing or prompt to move away
This is how I like to spend time off
As I begin each and every day.

## 94

God on high
Hear my prayer
In my need
You have always been there
You have been with me
You have sheltered and held
Lord, my God, my comfort
In You I find my home.
Certain of Your presence
Never fearing I am alone
Firm and confident in
You'll soon bring Your Kingdom.
Then on high
And here below
All creation and men
Will praise and know
What You have done
And continue to be in us all
United with one another
With You for ever more.

## 95

I hold his life in the palm of My hand
His every need I fully understand.
He that I now carefully hold,
Is more precious than silver or gold.
Worry not, he will be free,
He will come home to be with me.
I will comfort, I will soothe,
In these last days I'll not be cruel.
He will find rest here by my side,
All pain and suffering will subside.
Know each must pass from this world,
But as a butterfly with wings unfurled.
In flight such beauty can be seen,
Beauty beyond word, beyond your dreams.

## 96

When I am adrift and at a distance
You, Lord do not move at all
Staying nearer than a breath to me
You are whispering Your call.
When I am weary of life as it is
You, soothe without me knowing
Providing all I need or wish for
In countless wonderful blessings.
When I am sad looking there
To those who struggle and strive
You take what I have in service
So I may for others provide.
When any of us turn towards You
There is no falter, no pause
As no matter who we are, Lord
Children or adult are all Yours.

## 97

On days when there is so much pleasing
It's easy to be inspired and rejoice
At other times much more difficult
Even a smile having to be forced.

But no matter what, God is faithful
He lavishes His love upon all
Providing all that I ever need
And helps all blessings me to recall.

By messages of my loved ones
By sunrise and also of sunsets
With food, shelter and clothing
I am generously here blessed.

As I sleep now I am reminded
Of others who do not feel as I
And pray to God fervently now
He would respond to their cries.

That He would provide for all needs
Lifting each up and holding close
Giving reassurance and support
In the ways that are needed most.

May my response be evident too
In prayer but in action to take
In thankfulness of all I have
To another a real difference make.

Help me be she who doesn't moan
Who is positive and encouraging
Let there be a move by many
To cease relentless grumbling.

## 98

Day by day walking onward
Not knowing what's ahead
Yet heart lightened expectedly
Not weighed down with dread.

For each morning all is new
I need not feel troubled here
Of sin and wrong doing
Record has been made clear.

Righteous judge my God
Asks not for any recourse
Once confessed sincerely
Past forgiven for ever more.

This day I sing of praises
In voice and in my action
Thanking God for His grace
And all for me He has done.

Walking I raise my hands up
I give glory only to Him
Aware of redemption now
As this new day is dawning.

## 99

Lord within the day You are with me
From break of dawn to eventide
Never am I separated or alone
You are there close by my side.


Amongst the wakening of songbirds
I hear Your voice calling me too
A gentle whisper of greeting
As I enter the world anew.


The flower heads turn upwards
As sunrise emits its rays
And I turn to Your Word, Lord
To see what You have to say.


I hold Your book before me
Ready to receive Your wisdom
And then place it down again
Equipped for the day to begin.

At close of night I reflect too
Grateful for all You've bestowed
I sleep in peace and security
Enriched by what I've been told.


One day turns into another
Yet I do not tire - I am at ease
For with You each moment
I feel an incredible peace.

## 100

Praise You Lord for Your goodness
May all generations praise You
As I kneel here at Your feet
I pray that I will be ever faithful.
May my voice always be pleasing
In songs of everlasting joy
And my hands do only good, Lord
As with them gifting I employ.
May my thoughts be calm ones
Fearless and without anxiety
May I remember always, Lord
To praise you here, now and daily.

## 101

Lord, faithful, just and true
King of Kings, Lord of Lords
Grant that I may be faithful
With integrity answer your call.
May I discover new meaning
To Your Word in my hand
And learn how to apply it
In the ways You've planned.
Thank You that each day
You forgive and lead me on
Each step guiding carefully
Gently leading me along.
My praise to You is growing
In response to what I read
Realizing that in Your grace
You died to all redeem.
Day following day, dear Lord
You draw closer to my heart
And so I have but one option
To try to do my own part.
May I in humility speak now
With sincerity listen too
As I respond to Your call
Keep me safe and faithful.

## 102

Before the beginning of time
Your hands at work to create
Many options and opportunities
For action or to contemplate.
The days of my life etched
Upon the palm of your hand
The route to all I am to be
In some ways there planned.
Yet I have choice and reasoning
To do the things I here do
Though inevitably the good
Always brings me back to You.
The blessings are of You Lord
Timed perfectly for me I know
So that my spirit will develop
And my faith will also grow.
I thank you for your generosity
In grace giving so much to me
And ask that in days to come
You'd help me use all wisely.

## 103

Blessings are Yours, my Lord
As I pour out my praise
In loving thankfulness here
I offer You my full praise.
In reflecting on Your Word
And in Your presence rest
My cup overflows dear Lord
As You lavishly me bless.
On days I am quietened
Unable to know what to do
It is then I realise You're near
And wish me to not move.
With reassuring acceptance
You stoop down to enfold
Taking me in Your hands, Lord
You then carefully me hold.
I need do nothing at all
To just willingly receive
No expectation or demands
Simply as Your child, just be.

## 104

Upon the ground in my walking
I feel the support of Your Word
Above and beyond in the skies
Your firmament seen and heard.
With the rejoicing of creation
I join in escalating praise
As all awakens in newness
in the dawn of a new day.
There is no measure of thanks
For all I need You here bestow
Words fail to be enough here
In contrast felt to be hollow.
Graciously You listen with earnest
Hearing and knowing my heart
Eager to reassure my soul
And from limits set me apart.
For You even provide language
To exalt and adore You Lord
Leading me to Your throne
And nearer to You as I here walk.

## 105

I place before You my Lord, my God
All that is needed this hour, this day
Asking for Your grace and power
As You listen to what I hereby pray.
I thank You for your wisdom provided
For the guides and laws being set
But ask dear Lord for understanding
So the call to compliance would be met.
I pray for generosity of spirit too
For justice and wellbeing to prevail
And that together, united in hope
Our endeavours would not curtail.
Lord come with Your hand to channel
Take each of us to Your heart
Speak to us on all levels dear Lord
So everyone will play their part.
I place before You my Lord, my God
All that is needed this hour, this day
Asking for Your grace and power
As You listen to what I hereby pray.

## 106

In songs of everlasting joy
You call me to awaken to this day
With praise and thanksgiving
In worship to You I hereby pray.
Not wanting anything else, Lord
Than to place You as my focus
Knowing that for everything
I can in You put my whole trust.
May glory be Yours alone, Lord
My Creator, Redeemer and King
As with every heartbeat and step
I gladly to You this day sing.

## 107

At close of day when I look back
Upon the things that have gone
The blessing that means the most
Is the feeling that I here belong.

A sense of wellbeing within me
From my core out to my skin
A reassurance of my place now
Is where I am completely fitting.

There are many things to appreciate
People, needs met and time
But the one that helps me sleep
Is knowing within He is mine.

He the creator of my being
Who's known me all my life
Who takes upon Himself all
So that I need not ever strive.

He is my Lord and my God
Closer than the breath I breathe
The One who I thank each night
For all He graciously gives me.

**108**
With You Lord at my right hand
I need not fear rejection or foe
With you Lord at my right hand
I may valiantly forward go.
Victory mine when challenged
Will be my steadfast prayer
As I look to Your promise Lord
Of protection and of care.

## 109

Falsehood may be around me
Mouths that speak untruth so loud
But I am consoled that with You
Only Truth and goodness is found.
Accusers will fall and be found guilty
No foothold will there be for attack
Earth may be shaken in shadows
But in You my Lord I will nothing lack.
Dishonour will not be my clothing
As with my words I praise you in all
Grateful that in You I have everything
And need not look for anything more.

## 110

Lord, within the realms of this world
I have a place, yet am confused
How is it that You're there positioned
As if by me You are to be used.
If You are on my right hand, Lord
Then I realise You're perfectly placed
For there You will guide my actions
Demonstrating Your love and grace.
You will be my assurance, dear Lord
As You teach and I hereby learn
More of my place in the world
And of Your creativity be affirmed.
In awe and wonder and gratitude
I will become more likened to You
A person of patient contemplation
Who is loving and so very gentle.
Self will lower so as to be humble
With sincerity be calm and peaceful
Hereby appreciating every creature
Given to one another by You.

## 111

Your guidance is ever before me
Words from the past show the way
Yet in newness I read Your pages
As if all were written in recent days.

The wisdom is timeless in application
As applicable now as many years ago
It is as You have said so many times
Every moment to come You know.

As it was and is and ever shall be
Your understanding is consistent
Your faithfulness to all generations
The same and lovingly constant.

## 112

Lord, Your precepts are my guidance
In this life I am called to live
Of Your Word and Your Spirit
To my soul in Your grace You give.

I offer You my future days now
Asking You'd keep me safe from harm
Holding me close within Your heart
So as to rest in Your peace and calm.

May in my walk forward I be ready
To do all You now ask of me
With willingness of my spirit
With eyes that wish to really see.

May my hands become as Yours Lord
To aid others who may strive
As together in hope and assurance
Love, Your love, grows in my life.

## 113

As dawn turns to day
And day turns to dusk
I am reminded of Truth
The One I will ever Trust.
Day and night the same
Each no different to Him
Ever awake and present
To receive my praising.
When opportunity arises
Options and choices here
I ask God to guide me
Better actions to be clear.
I realise I am learning
Each step progress sure
So in time I'll Him reflect
And praise Him even more.

## 114

Amidst the change and sadness
There are glints of light to see
Hope for a future global love
To eradicate hunger and poverty.
It may seem unlikely ever
But why not, surely hope prevails
And upon the sea of equality
Justice and peace can indeed sail.
Onward to a world of infinity
Where nothing is ever impossible
That is what I hereby pray, Lord
As Your people are steered by You.
Take us to a place we love truly
Where everyone is valued complete
Bring Lord Your Kingdom soon
So we together may sit at Your feet.
Eager and willing to praise give
Faces shining with sun-like glow
As we in one another see Him
And You in wholeness really know.

## 115

Lord, in the moment and onwards
Encourage me and my openness
To be prepared to look and see
And my yearnings here confess.
May the way I look upon the world
Its creatures and my fellow man
Be where my hopes and dreams
Blending to make me who I am.

## 116

When life seems heavy burdened
And nothing of much makes sense
It is to You I need most of all
Knowing on You I can depend.

In silence I need no words
Just simply self reliance give up
So that You are free to hold me
And gently in Your palm cup.

My prayer for those who suffer
Is that they would to You release
All anxiety and depression
And receive Your love and peace.

## 117

Lord, a universal call to worship You
A proclamation on this new day
And as I prepare to join others
I hear Your voice gently now say,
"I am ever with you, truly
My steadfast love endures on
And I will be right by your side
On your path guiding you along.
There may be undulations
Trials and bumps on the road
But these will draw you closer
So of my love you'll really know.
Amongst the turns before you
I will teach more of my own self
It will be as only we two exist
As you will think of no one else.
Come, let us walk on together
Welcoming the day lying ahead
Mindful of each moment now
By My Word being here fed.
Seek, find and be nurtured
Into being who you are to be
Assured that I delight in you
Form of My own creativity.

Upon the pages of writing
Within the artwork produced
I am with you ever more
As you on me are focused.
You are the pen of the ready Writer
The artist of the One true God
And through all you share here
It shows others of My love.
Walk on with Me from shadows
So much more lies before you
And remember I am steadfast
My promises are always true."

## 118

To leave anywhere is daunting,
To move on to pastures new,
Yet, there's also excitement,
An anticipatory feeling too.

The unknown awaiting its beginning,
To become the present here and now,
Bidding me to be adventurous,
And more open to grow.

Amidst the concerns and challenge,
I know on God I can rely,
And though I move onwards
To the past I don't wave goodbye.

For the wisdom and learning to date,
Will go with me as I move on,
And as all is part of me too,
In the future all belongs.

There will be of course be lessons learnt,
And some things I'd rather leave behind,
But dwelling on these isn't healthy,
For my body, or soul or mind.

Along the path I'm about to travel,
I may reflect again on what's gone,
But feel little of any regrets,
Is in the present not welcome.

No wish to hold on to what hinders,
Or dream of things that couldn't be,
Accepting of who I am is all,
This is the job God has set for me.

To row my own canoe without ceasing,
To focus on Him and Him alone,
Until the day when all will make sense,
When at last I will dwell in His Home.

## 119

O Lord Your Word provides so much
Never ending in guidance and care
Upon the pages written oh so many
Promises and affirmations there.
Within my heart I take something
To ponder and bask in through time
Guarding each of Your blessings
As a treasure that has been made mine.
What do I give in response to You,
Lord?
There is only one think I can do
It is in thankful praise each day
Give my love in all measure to You.

## 120

**D**eprecation of self and others
**E**vading peace and eliciting hate
**A**voiding acceptance of difference
**F**alse accusing and judgemental
**N**ot truly wanting to understand
**E**ngaging in wrong doing
**S**peaking untruth and being prejudiced
**S**eeking to devalue someone
**This is deafness!**

## 121

Thanks be to You Lord
Keeper of my soul in rest and repose
Thanks be to You Lord
Who my inner thoughts always knows.

May Your wisdom and Truth flow
As I in stillness let self go
May Your wisdom and Truth flow
This day and in each tomorrow.

Let my growth in You be deepened
As I learn more of You here
Let my growth in You be deepened
As You make the path ahead clear.

Blessings abound as I receive
You are the One with whom I belong
Blessings abound as I receive
You are the One guiding me on.

Thanks be to You Lord
Keeper of my soul in rest and repose
Thanks be to You Lord
Who my inner thoughts always knows.

May Your wisdom and Truth flow
As I in stillness let self go
May Your wisdom and Truth flow
This day and in each tomorrow.

## 122

Peace be within your home
Where you pause for rest
Peace be within your heart
Accept God's sincere caress.
Peace be yours in all you do
Taking His hand proffered
Peace be with all you love
Each by His wings covered.

## 123

Mercy is Yours Lord the giver
Mine the one in need of receipt
Yet there're others too I realise
Ask for mercy also from me.
That I may be tender and humble
Not seek harm or scorn in disdain
But with eyes of Your compassion
Realise they and I are just the same.

## 124

Lord You provide great abundance
In Your provision in this our world
Bounty for soul and physical need Lord
You offer food aplenty and Your Word.

Yet we choose not to share equally
We are stifled and we hold back
Not willing to give to those in need
True compassion we seem to lack.

With pure grace Jesus stands here
Showing how life should really be
His prayers of supplication and love
Requesting that we would all truly see.

That all are equal and of great worth
No one greater than another at all
And that to step into the Light
If we listen is what Jesus calls.

To be one who graciously moves
And confronts the wronged and hurt
To be the voice of the accused
Not be in the shadows here turned.

Lord may I be ever thankful to you
Of Your gifts, grace and love
And when I see another in need
May I give them more than enough.

I am reminded but for Your grace
I could be walking in their shoes
And that each moment of time
We are each a reflection of You.

May I see Your face, dear Lord
And respond with servitude
In praise and thanksgiving I say
Here I am, here to be used.

**125**
Peace is the yearning of hearts
When troubles befall on all sides
It's then that I and others turn to
You and in Your presence abide.
In seeking You and comforted
Made mindful that You never rest
And whatever the circumstances
You teach and turn to us to bless.

## 126

Joy is the language of pleasure
Celebration of success and event
Blessings outpoured like harvest
Gifts and delights heaven sent.
Richness is the sweet jubilation
Tears of effort and recourse
Not for sorrow but of gladness
In service that is like Yours.

## 127

Lord, Your generosity is limitless
It is this I rely on and ask for
In the silence of the night ahead
Please listen to hearts that call.
Come to them with great power
Provide all that each needs
Remove any hurts and sorrow
As souls with peace You feed.
Grant release from bondage
Of all that holds another back
Allow minds and bodies console
And release from all attacks.
Cover each with Your wings Lord
Restore in and with sleep this night
So that as darkness fades
All will be ready for the Light.
Thank You Lord for promises
Of presence and love always
Oh that I would sing out Lord
My words of everlasting praise.
In slumber and in quiet now
I lift in prayer to Your throne
Hearts of others that here call
Along with this... my own.

## 128

Lord, may my hands be willing
This day to be used by You
A willingness within my heart
Be ready to serve others too.

Action and response positive
Ears alert to those who speak
Compassion for the weary
Always to You mild and meek.

May this day be one blessed
As to You I graft my soul
In each moment here passing
Your wisdom within You'd sow.

In each of the days yet to be
May I be fruitful for You Lord
Guided by Your Spirit here
Nurtured by Your holy Word.

Onwards and upwards
Grounded with deep roots
A canopy of protection above
With ever growing shoots.

When at last I am at peace
May my life have been of good
In which offered opportunities
To love You I'm assured I took.

May this new day be fruitful
With kind words, acts of grace
In everyone I meet hereon
May I see in them Your face.

## 129

Silence can be a weapon
Or a place to resign oneself to good
Better not to speak out in anger
To in quietness focus on love.
Not the wicked to attack verbally
But wait and in quiet repose
Rely on Your judgement, Lord
And on Your justice trust bestow.

**130**
More than those who watch for morning
I hope upon You my Lord, My God
Deep the yearnings of my own heart
As I seek only with it to You love.
Cast out all my ways of not pleasing
Grant me in Your power redemption
Bring Your forgiveness and grace
And so doing my soul's completion.

## 131

Lord within the noise of devastation
Amidst the cries of horror and of fear
May You be the One to whom we turn
Our God ever present and ever near.


Silence the voices of anger and outrage
Those that shout and themselves hurt
Come, Lord in Your power and wisdom
Like a mighty wind and ocean surge.


Cover all nations with Your protection
Teach each that in You we now must
In quiet of our hearts respond sincerely
Placing our lives and our world in Your trust.


Only with You will there by any meaning
All foundation on You is Your call
Lord, in Your grace come and save
Generously provide for one and all.

This is Your Kingdom at the ready
Opening itself to Your residence now
A contrite people with true desire
To before Your throne to hereby bow.


Help, Lord and be amongst us
Guide and show each the Way
This the yearning of Creation manifest
This my own prayer for this day.

## 132

Again Your Word tells me of provision
That in everything You give so much
Not just what is needed though, Lord
In abundance there is more than enough.
You ask only that hands be laid open
That hearts be flesh and not of stone
And that I acknowledge Your Holy Spirit
Ever beside me so I am never alone.
Onward we will walk together, Lord
Along the path You've made ready for me
You will be my Light along the Way
Making the turns ahead easier to see.
There may be some hesitation, yes,
But pauses will surely help me too
For it will be then that I move closer
And acknowledge reliance on You.
May this day be the first of so many
When I can rejoice and surely know
That I am Yours and You are mine
Just as You destined it to be so.

**133**
Union is the call of all creation
Separateness to man dissolved, gone
Together being complete and good
Is where everything knows it belongs.
Division is not healthy or of merit
For as it was in the beginning
Unity is God's wish for our planet.

## 134

Blessings and worship is asked for
Acknowledgement of who is Lord
All within this world of creation
In blessing of God all are now called.
None shall sleep and not be awakened
All will arise with one voice of praise
With gratitude and thanksgiving
Let voices lift to heaven's holy place.

## 135

All creations that on earth do dwell
In sky and also within the waters and sea
Singing praise of You their Lord on high
Is how God yearns all to return to be.
Bondage and captivity is to be removed
Freedom for all is in His plan, our hands
Each one as is able must be prepared
To play their own part – to take a stand.
Let those who have ears truly listen
Let those who have eyes completely see
Let the blessing of enlightenment, Lord
Be at work now, and start here with me.

## 136

Steadfast is the love of God
Steadfast and honest and true
Enduring throughout generations
As predictable as the sun and moon.
Amidst the anguish of nations
Even here there will be His hope
The wilderness only short term
Within which anyone need cope.
He will raise a mighty arm in victory
He'll sustain and honour each one
As He bids all as He then rescues
To into His own Kingdom to come.

## 137

Sorrow of all that is around us
Yet also the rock on which to stand
The voice that has power over all
Is close with His victorious hand.
There may not be singing here
Tears of sadness be the only lament
Yet within the coldness and darkness
It is not God who drives torment.
He too is filled with wish for better
The world as He wants it to be
And in this I am reminded here
That all change starts with me.

## 138

A new song will be our voice now
The past will wither and fade away
As the Lord's greatness is voiced
In what all people do and now say.
Weep now and lament with sadness
For all that has gone – only right
But remember in Jubilee sing out
That God was there in the plight.
Courage He gave to those broken
Peace was the rest which sustained
Never from the midst of troubles
Did He leave you or any forsake.

## 139

I am fearfully and wonderfully made
My being extra-ordinary in many ways
My life ahead already recorded there
Within the book of my earthly days.
I am excited as I now anticipate
The path that is now ahead of me
Ups and downs and turns in route
As I explore and enjoy discovery.
There will be sadness, I know
But more important will be hope
And the knowledge I am not alone
So no matter what I will surely cope.
Onwards I take the next steps here
Knowing more love and wisdom
Aided by God's presence alongside
I am His and He is mine for certain.

## 140

A thankfulness of hope abounds
Within a heart that is contrite here
As things of the past are put behind
My soul and mind are made now clear.
A thankfulness of love comes too
As with grace I am filled to others give
Servanthood becoming a life to live.
Joyfulness is my own reward
As in trust I am able to move on
Knowing that He is with me always
As together He and I - we belong.

## 141

Lord help me to look to Your eyes
To see that in them Your love reflected back
Lord help me to look into Your eyes
To see that in them no one is ever bad.

Lord help me to look into Your eyes
And then to see another as You do
Lord help me to look into Your eyes
And respond to another in love too.

Lord help me to understand others
That their sadness is not because of me
But that they have not asked to look
And with Your eyes to really see.

Help me to remember all are precious
And need a helping hand and care
Lord when I look and they look too
May each in the other see You there.

## 142

The light of Your goodness surrounds me
Everywhere I turn it and You are there
Within the pages of Your word dear Lord
It is as if to You are drawn even closer.
As I turn the soft paper back and forth
Reading and re-reading what's there written
It is as though it's for the first time again
Like a lover of You I am now smitten.
Eager to learn more of Your wisdom
I return to spend time more frequently
Somehow trying to catch up on all missed
Wanting You to be more a part of me.
Thankfulness consumes my being
Realising opportunity I'm provided with
Your continual Light shining on me
Guiding each moment that I now live.

## 143

Stilling me, holding me
So I can sit here at Your side
No place to rush to or think about
Simply with You I can abide.

Gracious is Your love to us
An abundance coming to bless
As together here gathered
We each with you now rest.

Glorified in Heaven above my Lord
Angels there and below here sing
Praises of adoration and thankfulness
With Your Host I too now bring.

Celebration is loud and affirming
As one voice joins another
A crescendo of jubilation
Like a canopy of joy covering over.

Now in the silence I am content
Nothing to distract my soul's focus
The refreshment of time set aside
Of recharging peace and quietness.

Somehow the quiet is shortened
More of Your stillness I need
As my heart's desire is lit
To without sound for longer be.

I may not be able to linger
But I can take great console
That in my mind's eye within
A calmness I'll continue to know.

Until next time dear Lord
When I will come and repose
I celebrate with Your angels
In peace and thanks so joyous.

## 144

As set like an army fueled by love
You bestow blessings upon me to cope
And deep within my heart You place
An abundance of grace and of hope.
Your words provide songs of honour
As Truth is the battle cry loud and clear
Marking the passage of time passing
As to Your Kingdom all grows near.
Soon will be deliverance and security
When the whole earth praises You alone
Assured of salvation and belonging
In a world that You have made home.
No longer any distance between us
Union and acceptance of all so clear
We will rise up with arms of jubilation
Announcing indeed Jesus Himself is here.

## 145

God of compassion with hands holding up
We Your children encapsulated by love.
Only able to do what is pleasing and right
Because Your Spirit within us is our guide.
Equipped and gifted with all that we need
To act justly and love mercy we're freed.
Serving without any need for reward
As we say humbly, thank you, dear Lord.

*elle*

## 146

Lord of compassion and of truth
Be with me this day I here ask
That I would be as You'd wish
In each of my every day tasks.
If when walking I see a need
May I not deliberately turn away
Give me the grace to remember
I could be she in need one day.
In each of the steps I move now
May I follow those of Your own
Making Your example of love
Within my heart a secure home.
Where it will flourish and develop
Second nature being my service
Eagerly providing support for others
My hands being as Yours, Jesus.

## 147

There amidst the friendships
That are nurtured as these
There's a deep understanding
An acceptance and a peace.
No one is more special, no
Each has a place and gift
As we for just a short time
Each week share the life we live.
Thank You Lord for one another
For friendships and for care
The reassurance of this space
Of true fellowship to savour.
Lord I ask You to bless each
In the coming days as we part
May we all know Your presence
In our own and each others' hearts.

## 148

Praise of thanksgiving uplifted
To the heights, along with angels goes
A wonderful chorus of all creation
As all His now to Him draw close.

Sustained in a choir resounding
Are the echoes of his love and grace
As each in turn is before their Lord
Lost in wonder they are amazed.

Joyous and not lacking vigour
All with voice of one clear accord
Announcing God's universal glory
As of the world He is made Lord.

## 149

Faith has been blessed with goodness
All peoples and places God now edifies
Joy, love and praises rise up
As together affirmed they cry
Gathered and united are all men
None are desolate or abandoned
As royal priesthood so now named
And their King hereby crowned.

**150**

Silence within
Like a stirring

Silence within
Like my hoping

Silence within
All consuming

Silence within
Is my praising.

# Acknowledgements

The poetry included in *On Eagle's Wings* is also available alongside beautiful photographs by Susan Williams. Published as a series titled *Hymns of Hope* 5 Kindle books encourage pauses and reflection.

My thanks to Sharon Walsh for proof reading – your eye for detail is such a blessing to me, as is your friendship spanning over 50 years.

I am blessed by many friends who encourage me to write and publish; I thank each and every one.

I dedicate *On Eagle's Wings* to Angela Kipling as she rests in peace.

*Upon Eagle's wings you raise me up*
*Taking me to a place far off*
*Prompting to leave all burdens*
*There at the foot of the cross.*
*Come my child you whisper*
*Your tenderness calming me*
*And holding me close we saur*
*Beyond the green canopy.*
*Nothing of earth ties us down*
*Nor weighs heavily within*
*Letting go we fly high above*
*Liberated upon the wing.*

## Other publications by Kate Brumby

*In the Palm of His Hand*
©2019 Published by Daisa & Co Publishing
A collection of 60 poems available in hardback, e-book, and audio.

*No Ordinary King*
©2019 Published by Kindle Direct Publishing
A Christmas themed anthology of 15 poems available in paperback and e-book

*His Guiding Hand*
©2020 Published by Daisa & Co Publishing
A memoir including over 120 poems available in paperback.

*God of Detail*
©2020 Published by Kindle Direct Publishing
The first 52 pages of *His Guiding Hand* available as e-book

*Poetry of the Sole*
©2020 Published by Kindle Direct Publishing
Reflections and poetry with photographs by Susan Williams
Available in paperback and e-book.

*Touch of Remembrance*
©2020 Published by Kindle Direct Publishing
Short story available as e-book

*What the Eye Does Not See*
©2020 Published by Kindle Direct Publishing
Short story available as e-book

Kate also has 7 journal notebooks available featuring poems from her collection *In the Palm of His Hand*. These are available via Amazon and also via her Etsy Shop Poetry247
https://www.etsy.com/uk/shop/Poetry247

Kate is always pleased to connect with readers. You can access her social media platforms via her website:

www.katebrumby.co.uk

@PoetBrumby
@Poetry247

@PoetBrumby

@Kate_Brumby_Poet_Author

Printed in Great Britain
by Amazon